Table of Contents

The Importance of Bread
Why You Should Make Your Own Bread Instead of Buying
Ingredients
Equipment
The Bread Making Process
Leavening
RECIPES
    Master Bread Recipe
    Baguette
    Ciabatta
    Bagel
    Bretzel
Entire Grain Bread
    Wholemeal Sandwiches
    Whole Grain Loaf
    Multi Cereal Bread
Special Bread
    Olive Bread
    Walnuts Bread
    Pumpkin Bread
    Tricolor Bread
Classic Bread
    Grissini
    Piadina
    Original Focaccia
Sweetened Bread
    Brioches Bread
    Banana Bread
    Raisin Bread
PIZZA RECIPES
    Pizza Dough
PIZZA TOPPING
    Marinara

Margherita
Bufala
Emilia Romagna
Lombardia
Trentino
Liguria
Roma
Sicilia
Puglia
Abruzzo
Piemonte
Toscana
MEASUREMENTS CONVERSION

The Importance of Bread.

Bread is an essential food prepared by baking a dough of flour and water. It's one of the world's earliest foods. The boundless mixes of different flours and differing proportions of components, has led to a variety of types, shapes, sizes, and textures readily available worldwide. Bread baking is a chemical process that involves the usage of wheat gluten (flour), yeast for increasing, a sweetener to feed the yeast and warm water to provide a wet environment for the yeast and to bind the other active ingredients together. It might be leavened (aerated) by a variety of different procedures ranging from making use of naturally taking place microbes to high-pressure artificial aeration throughout preparation and baking, or might be left unleavened. A wide range of ingredients may be used to flavor bread and to create countless variations.

Bread may be served in different forms as any meal of the day, consumed as a treat and is even used as an active ingredient in other cooking preparations.

Here are some crucial nutritional facts about bread:

- Calcium

White bread is strengthened with calcium and four medium pieces each day would offer over 30% of the advised day-to-day consumption of calcium, which we require every day to keep healthy bones and teeth.

- Fiber

Bread, specifically wholemeal, is a source of dietary fiber that helps to keep our digestive system healthy, assists in reducing the amount of blood sugar and cholesterol, which makes us feel better and lighter.

- Protein

Bread is a low-fat source of protein that our bodies need to renew and grow.

- Iron

White bread is strengthened with iron. Iron is necessary for energy and concentration, a healthy immune system and healthy blood.

- Vitamins & Other Minerals

Bread consists of a wide variety of minerals and vitamins, including B group vitamins thiamine (B1), Niacin (B3), which are very important for launching energy from food and maintenance of healthy skin, eyes and nails.

- Energy

Bread is reasonably low in calories. A typical medium piece of white bread includes 77 calories, brown includes 72 calories and wholemeal contains 79 calories.

- Fat

Bread is a low-fat food. A bread averagely contains 0.6 g of fat, brown bread consists of 0.7 g and wholemeal contains 0.9 g. Just take care what you place on it and adhere to healthy options for spreads and toppings.

- Sugar

A lot of breads are low in sugar, which is very important for healthy teeth and maintaining a healthy weight.

Why You Should Make Your Own Bread Instead of Buying

Nothing is more rewarding than the aroma of newly baking bread originating from the oven and wafting through your home. It resembles saying welcome without a word being spoken. There truly is no secret to bread baking and it is most likely among the simplest things to do, although the majority of people might think that baking bread is an uphill struggle. It takes time, but it's worth it.

If you can bake a loaf of bread, you can best adapt it to your personal tastes.

Homemade Bread is Healthier

It's much healthier to bake your own bread instead of purchasing bread, which contains chemical additives, hydrogenated oils, unhealthy preservatives, and fattening sweeteners. When you bake your own bread, you never have to stress about these "covert threats" or chemicals in bread. Instead, you can control every active ingredient that goes into your bread, and you'll understand exactly how it is processed and created. There are lots of other terrific rewards for baking homemade entire wheat bread, and I'll go into every one below.

Homemade Bread Tastes Better Than Store-Bought

No argument here. Everyone I've asked agrees that the taste of homemade bread far surpasses that of store-bought bread, (some have even said they might taste the chemicals in the store-bought bread and hated it). Taste is a big deal for many people, and since everybody wishes to consume yummy meals, you can't fail by baking your own bread.

Homemade Bread Saves You Money

It's much more affordable to purchase all the ingredients for making bread separately, than buying them currently made into bread. You can quickly save some money every month, by baking your own bread. This is particularly true if you buy as a lot of your bread ingredients as you can in the bulk department of a grocery store. A whole bag of entire wheat flour (enough to make 4 to 6 loaves) is not that expensive. This is simply one example of how cheap baking your own bread is.

Homemade Bread is Lower in Fat

My preferred reason for baking bread is that, if you bake the best kind of bread (like whole-wheat bread) it can be a terrific way to help you lose pounds or maintain a healthy weight. Most store-bought bread contains lots of fats since of all the additionals that big-scale manufacturers stuff their bread with. Makers do this to provide their bread longer service life and to make the bread look more appealing so they'll get more customers to purchase their bread. But if you bake your own entire wheat bread, you'll have a truly wholesome bread that will assist you in attaining the healthy body, goal weight and the life you prefer.

Ingredients

1. FLOUR

It is the main ingredient used to make bread. It gives structure to baked items, but different baked products demand different structural supports. Pick the best flour for the best job and you're a long way toward baking success. Pick the wrong flour and you're courting trouble. Protein material is the main differentiator in flours. High-protein wheat ranges (10 to 14 percent protein) are classed as "tough wheat." Low-protein wheats (5 to 10 percent) are called "soft wheat." Put simply: more protein equals more gluten, strength and more power translates to more volume and chewy texture. The dough made from high protein flour is more flexible (spreads) and more elastic (better maintains its shape). Unless identified "whole-wheat," all flour is white flour: that is, milled from the starchy, inner part of the wheat kernel, called the endosperm.

Types of flour

- 00 Flour

With a protein material of 12 to 14 percent, 00 flour is the strongest of all flours, supplying the most structural support. This is specifically crucial in yeasted breads, where a strong gluten network is required to consist of the CO_2 gases produced during fermentation. The extra protein creates better volume and a chewy crumb.

- Manitoba flour

The main characteristic of Manitoba flour is its resistance, which, with its high protein content and significant water absorption, makes it suitable for more complex recipes. It's used to prepare specialties such as focaccia, pizza and certain types of bread, such as delicious baguettes or focaccia.

Manitoba flour is high in glutenin and gliadin: two insoluble proteins that, when in contact with water, produce gluten and make the dough more elastic and consistent. This means it is more suitable for the bread making process or for the production of products that require a long soaking time.

Guaranteed to be easy to work with, at least compared to whole wheat flour, this type of flour is perfectly suited to the bread making routine and is therefore used to make bread and pizza. However, since it has medium-sized granules with a higher bran content, it is less soluble than refined flour, making gluten less effective. Consequently, the dough is not as elastic and stable, but it is still suitable for a multitude of preparations, especially dough with short and long preparation times.

- **Whole-Grain Flour**

This flour still contains the external kernel of the wheat, also understood as wheat bacterium. If you wish to add whole-wheat flour to a recipe, substitute as much as half of the all-purpose flour with whole wheat; any more than that and your baked excellent may be too tough.

- **Gluten-Free Flours**

There is a broad range of gluten-free flours readily available today, made from all sorts of starches, grains and nuts. Many people mix a few various non-wheat flours to mimic all-purpose wheat flour for baking. A little percentage of xanthan gum is sometimes included to help replicate the chewiness generally related to gluten. Seek advice from the particular recipe or packaging for details on how to replace it for wheat flour in your favorite baking recipes.

The Very Best Method To Measure Flour

Do you scoop your flour using the measuring cup? You could be accidentally including up to 20% more flour to your recipe if you are! Flour settles and compacts in the bag or storage container, so when you scoop, you're including unwanted flour. That implies drier, crumblier baked products.

The most precise way to determine flour is to weigh it on a kitchen area scale. Location a bowl on the scale and tare it to no, then add the amount of flour you need: 1 cup of all-purpose flour = 120 grams or 4 1/4 ounces.

If you don't have a scale, then use the spoon-in-and-level-off method: Fluff flour with a fork to loosen it and then spoon it into a determining cup and level it off with a straight edge like the back of a knife.

2. WATER

Water is the most frequently utilized liquid in bread making. It assists and dampens the flour in forming the dough. It likewise assists in the baking process. Water performs these three primary functions in the bread dough.

- Assists to hydrate and dampen the insoluble proteins.
- Distributes the yeast among the entire dough.
- Binds the flour and other components into a dough.

The amount of water in the dough significantly affects the rate of fermentation. The speed of fermentation is higher in ferment and dough process as compared to sponge and dough procedure, which have an increasing level of hydration.

As the fermentation time increases, it becomes necessary to reduce the water to effect a greater ripening of the dough. The quantity of water present will likewise greatly affect the texture of the last dough acquired.

3. YEAST

Yeast is a single cell microorganism which triggers the leavening in the dough. It transforms the natural sugar in the flour into tiny bubbles of carbon dioxide trapped in the dough. During baking, these bubbles expand to offer the texture and lightness to the dough.

The perfect temperature for yeast to act is 25°C. There are different type of yeast.

Instant Yeast

It is produced comparable to active dry yeast, however with more porous granules that do not require the reactivation step. This leavener operates in about half the time of active dry yeast. It can be utilized interchangeably with active dry yeast when baking in an oven. Instant yeast is normally used for desserts, where the large quantity of sugars and fats make the dough heavy and difficult to increase with natural yeasts.

Brewer's yeast

At first produced from the fermentation of beer (hence the name), brewer's yeast is a kind of single-cell mushroom that replicates in the presence of sugars and oxygen.

The benefit of beer yeast, therefore, is that of obtaining leavened doughs in a brief time, but to the detriment of aroma and digestibility life. To get more digestible and much better-tasting items, you can decrease the amount of yeast, increasing the rising times. Remember, however, that a greater maturation of the dough will require a greater quantity of protein (or gluten), for that reason, weak flours are not ideal for this type of leavening: utilize strong flours!

Mother yeast

Sourdough is generally a mix of water and flour acidified by a complex of yeasts and lactic bacteria efficient in starting the fermentation procedure.

Bread created with sourdough will not only be more aromatic and more digestible, but will likewise stay soft and fresh much longer!

Biga and poolish

Poolish is a semi-liquid pre-mix (80-120% hydration, i.e. with 80-120% water compared to flour: 80-120 ml of water is used every 100 g of flour) gotten by blending water, yeast and flour and left to rest for a period of time that can vary from 2-4 hours to 18-24 hours.

The biga is a semi-solid pre-mix (40-60% hydration) acquired by mixing flour, yeast and water and delegated rest for a duration of time that can differ from 8-10 to 36-48 hours.

Both need to be prepared with strong flours and they generally differ according to the quantity of yeast and the increasing temperature. Whether you use the poolish or the biga, when the pre-dough has actually been fermented, the other active ingredients need to be added based on the dish, then continue with the typical leavening.

4. SALT

The primary function of salt is to control the action of yeast as it decreases the fermentation process.

Salt mainly carries out the following functions:

- Imparts flavour;

- Offers stability to gluten;

- Controls the rate of fermentation; and

- Affects the crust colour and crumb, due to manage on the rate of fermentation.

More salt or less salt will negatively affect the final item.

5. SUGAR

Sugar is the main food that yeast eats to yield alcohol and carbon dioxide. Except for lactose, yeast can break down all other sugars in the dough, either naturally in flour or as a supplement to sugar, mainly sucrose or often maltose.

The flour contains about two and a half to three percent sugars from sucrose and maltose. This suffices for the yeast in the preliminary parts of the fermentation. Like salt, excessive sugar or less sugar will affect the dough texture.

6. Extra Virgin Olive Oil - EVO

It is utilized to supply flavour and softness to the texture. Different kinds of fats are used for various breads such as olive oil for focaccia (Italian bread).

Equipment

Important tools that are relevance:

- Baking tray
- Baking stone
- Bench scraper
- Bowl scraper
- Bread knife
- Cleaning up brushes
- Cooling rack
- Scale - however truly, this one is extremely essential
- Containers or little plastic food storage containers
- Kitchen area towels or cling wrap
- Mixing bowls
- Thermometers (Oven thermometer, Probe thermometer and Ambient temperature level thermometer)
- Rolling pin

Comprehending the Tools

Baking tray - We will use the tray for your first loaf and whole wheat bread. Option to vary for many dough recipes and a great addition to any kitchen area

Baking stone - Used to make pizzas and baguettes, but useful for other types of baking.

Bench Scraper – It is an indispensable tool. Essential to cut doughs and pull doughs off of countertops.

Bowl Scraper - A bowl scraper may be the most widely used tool and it comes in all shapes and sizes. I like a couple of shapes on hand for all different types of bowl shapes and dough consistencies. The orange one covered in silicone is excellent for actually damp doughs, while the plastic ones withstand more rigid doughs

Bread Knife - Get an excellent serrated knife. The worst is attempting to cut into a loaf of bread and having to crush it due to your knife. Use long sawing actions and go slow, let the knife and gravity do the work, you do not require to apply loads of pressure.

Cleaning Up Brushes - One for your meals, and one for your fingers and nail beds. Sponges are pretty worthless when it pertains to tidying up doughy messes, the cleaning brush works better and faster.

Cooling Rack - A place where you can put all the wonderful bread you take out of the oven or the stove. We will use this rack to ensure even cooling of the crust with plenty of air flowing through all sides of the dough.

Scale - We will utilize this to measure our ingredients. We determine the weight of active ingredients since it is even more precise to measure a weight 500g of flour than it is to try and measure the volume of 2 1/4 cups of flour. Remember, baking is all about precision and consistency. Bakers like to know precisely just how much of each ingredient they are including to their ferments and mixes, bread making is actually a science where small amounts of active ingredients may affect our resultant loaves considerably.

Containers or little plastic food storage containers - Great for keeping starters in, doing small pre-ferments for sourdough, pizza, and baguettes. They are reusable and resistant!

Kitchen Towels - We use kitchen towels in great deals of ways, so stock up on at least 4 or 5 simply for bread making.

Mixing Bowls - A great mix of bowls with covers and clear bowls are downright important. The doughs spend a great deal of time hanging out in blending bowls, fermenting and rising. You will usually use at least 2 blending bowls for each recipe.

Thermometer - Temperature level is a big consider bread making. We will utilize thermometers to make certain our ambient temperatures aren't affecting our dough increase too significantly. When dough becomes too cold or too hot, it affects your increase time. I suggest getting an oven thermometer, a probe thermometer, and an ambient temperature thermometer.

Rolling pin – Simple but essential tool that make your life easier for stretching the dough.

The Bread Making Process

1. Scaling

Before starting the bread making process, it is essential to collect all of your active ingredients and measure them properly. Determining components by weight is a lot more accurate method to measure and is the favored technique for bread making.

2. Mixing

Now that we've got our active ingredients, it's time to mix them! Although mixing sounds simple (and obviously, at the core it is!) it's an extremely essential action. When making bread, it greatly assists to blend the dry ingredients first (with no filling however, such as raisins, etc.) before including the wet components. Mixing requires no effort as long as there are no wet ingredients.

Blending ensures all active ingredients are spread out over the bread evenly. It ensures yeast is spread out through the whole dough and therefore makes it evenly fluffy. It guarantees the salt is mixed through uniformly. Because excessive salt will avoid development of yeast, it prevents (regional) inhibition of yeast development.

Even mixing should be done with care. If the wetness included is too hot, yeast can be eliminated. Boiling water above 40°C will kill the yeast, so only use warm water.

3. Hydrating & Resting

This step is not fully needed, however when blending by hand or using a great deal of whole wheat flour, this can absolutely assist. This phase includes leaving the dough mix just like that for about 30 minutes.

During this resting duration, the flour hydrates, more particularly the starch and gluten of the flour are hydrated by water. Water seeps into the grains and will relax the molecules. It takes longer for water to take a trip through if a flour has more fibers and grainy parts (as for coarse wholemeal flour). Often a dough is softer and more flexible after resting. It makes it much easier to knead in the next action.

4. Kneading

Kneading introduces air into the dough. These air bubbles are essential for producing an airy bread. Despite the fact that yeast will produce gas throughout rising, it has been found that no new air bubbles are necessarily formed during rising. Instead, existing air bubbles grow. Creating these air pockets during kneading is vital. It's these air pockets that enable bread to end up being fluffy.

Kneading by hand

Kneading by hand needs practice and persistence. There are numerous methods for doing so, repeatedly smashing the dough on the counter, pulling it apart and many more.

Electric mixers

The kind of mixer matched for your requirements mostly depends upon the quantities of bread you make. If you're a house baker with max. 1-2 breads per baking session, I would suggest a regular stand mixer with the dough hook. I would not advise purchasing the mini version. Some bread doughs can be pretty hard to knead for the routine mixer already, I do not think the mini will make it.

One size bigger would be the professional variation of the stand mixer. It isn't that much bigger, but does likewise have a bit more power.

5. Proofing/ Bulk fermentation

The moment a dough has been made, it is all set for its first increase, also called bulk or very first fermentation.

Yeast have an ideal development temperature. They don't grow (or are really sluggish) at temperature levels below this growth temperature or above this growth temperature. In the refrigerator, yeast still produce gas, however, it's at a lower rate than at room temperature.

Besides controlling the temperature level, humidity likewise plays a crucial role at this moment. If you don't want the dough to get dry, you can prevent this by properly covering the bowl in which the dough is increasing. Make sure though that the dough does not touch the cover (remembering it will still grow), to prevent sticking. Usually, you can do this first proofing period in your mixing bowl, which safeguards the dough against drying out on the sides and makes it simple to cover. A fantastic method to cover your bowls is to use a shower cap, it's water-resistant and puff up so the dough can grow without it touching the cap.

Proofing does not need expensive devices, your bowls, towels and plastic foil (beneath the towels) work great.

6. Shaping

Once the first fermentation is ended up the dough needs to be taken from the bowl you're proven it in and divide into the required dough sizes. Using a dough scraper here will make your life a lot much easier, I say so from personal experience, it will help to avoid your fingers being all doughy even prior to you started shaping. Shaping the bread after the first rising process assists to create a better structure of the bread.

Before forming the bread, the newly risen bread should be pushed down once again and air bubbles must be eliminated. This will provide the bread another opportunity to rise again because the yeast is fed again with sugars in the dough. It avoids too big bubbles from forming.

After the air has been pressed out you form your bread. Throughout forming, you identify the final kind of bread you're making, whether it's long, round or square.

7. Scoring

This is likewise an action that is often overlooked! By scoring the bread, it has more area to open!

You can do scoring with anything sharp. You can even use special scoring knives.

8. Baking

Baking is where your dough ends up being a bread. During baking a great deal of things happen. Of all, the yeast gets one last development spike –If you've scored it well, this causes the loaf to broaden.

The temperature level of your oven affects how your bread ends up. A higher heat will give a darker crust more quickly. If the bread is very large, the exterior may be almost black, whereas the inside is not yet cooked. Greater heats offer thinner and softer crusts, whereas lower heats give thicker crusts. The lower heat makes you have to bake your bread longer, so more moisture evaporates. This wetness evaporation is necessary to make a crispy crust.

9. Cooling & Eating

Nothing much to state here! The most important part of the bread making procedure. Take the bread out of the oven. Let it cool (slicing hot bread is a recipe for catastrophe, it will break down so easily) and enjoy!

Leavening

For those who are not acquainted with dough and bread making, one of the worst predicaments concerns leavening, so let's begin with the most diverse concerns. How much yeast to use? Is it better to increase at room temperature level or in the refrigerator? Above all, with all these variables, how do leavening times change?

This chapter is made especially for all of you who approach bread making, to answer these and other concerns you have most likely asked yourself. Obviously, I will provide general indications based on my experience, some initial notions from which to get a first concept. Then, it will be up to you to practice, experiment, and evaluate what your technique for excellence is.

I will begin with a question that will appear weird to some: what is leavening?

The response is easy: leavening results from a chemical reaction that transforms glucose into co2 and ethyl alcohol. This carbon dioxide will remain caught in the glutinic mesh, forming the bubbles, which will trigger the increase in volume and make the dough soft. The co2 will evaporate throughout cooking.

This is why the choice of flour is essential and why flours with little gluten (such as rye or barley) or no gluten (such as corn or rice) increase harder.

Store yeast in the fridge

Contrary to what many think, rest in the fridge is not a leavening stage. When you store below 8-10°C the yeast metabolism starts to be inhibited.

Normally you rest dough in the refrigerator for timing reasons or to slow the leavening.

Yeasts and Leavening: Amounts and Times

Let's get to the primary doubt, that is, the ratio between the amount of yeast and the rising times.

I'll start by explaining that whether you use sourdough or brewer's yeast, the rising times do not simply depend upon the quantity of yeast utilized. There are numerous variables, beginning with the room temperature level (the optimum would be a continuous temperature level of 28-30°C, without modifications or currents), travelling through the type of flour, the "additional" active ingredients of the dough (the seasonings - from salt to candied fruit to treated meats to dried fruit - they weigh down the dough and hinder its rising), the percentage of water.

Here, schematically reported, two tables that explain the conversion of the leavening times in relation to the quantity of yeast (beer yeast in the first, mother yeast in the second). Remember that these are indicative times, which consider just to a particular degree the numerous external factors.

Rising timetable for 1 kg of 00/0 flour mixed with brewer's yeast

Fresh Brewer's Yeast	Air temperature	In the fridge
22-25 g	2 (1,5-3) hours	4 (2,5-5) hours
18-20 g	4 (2,5-5) hours	6 (4-8) hours
14-16 g	6 (4-8) hours	9 (6-12) hours
10-12 g	8 (5-10) hours	12 (10-15) hours
6-8 g	10 (6-12) hours	15 (12-18) hours
1-4 g	12 (8-15) hours	20 (18-24) hours

Warning: with dry brewer's yeast, the times may increase. Read the instructions on the package as many dry yeasts must be activated before use. In principle **1 g of dry yeast = 3 g of fresh yeast.**

Rising timetable for 1 kg of 00/0 flour mixed with sourdough

Sourdough	Air temperature	In the fridge
250-300 g	5 (4-7) hours	9 (6-12) hours
200-220 g	8 (7-10) hours	12 (10-15) hours
150-180 g	11 (10-13) hours	15 (12-18) hours
100-120 g	14 (13-16) hours	18 (15-20) hours
50-80 g	17 (16-19) hours	20 (18-24) hours
10-30 g	20 (19-24) hours	24 (22-28) hours

What Affects Leavening

Basically, the primary aspects influencing yeast activity are:

- Temperature. Constantly remember that yeasts are living beings: at high temperatures (50 - 60°C), these bacteria pass away in a really short time (therefore, it is impossible that a prepared dough can continue to increase). Just as temperatures near to 0°C, on the other hand, cause a slowdown from fermentation. This is why yeast ought to never ever be utilized cold in the fridge once brought back to room temperature level: in this way, the cells are enabled to reactivate and revitalize. Within specific limitations, the ambient temperature significantly influences the activity of the yeast: the cold inhibits its action, the heat accelerates it. If you put the dough in the refrigerator, the leavening decreases considerably until it almost stops. Vice versa, if you blend with a temperature level of about 28-30°C, the leavening will be much faster.

- Presence of oxygen. Yeasts can metabolize sugars in the presence of oxygen, transforming basic sugars into carbon dioxide, water and cell mass, or in the lack of oxygen, producing ethyl alcohol and carbon dioxide. Generally, both circumstances take place: in the first phase, the yeast consumes all the oxygen, then the alcoholic fermentation begins.

- Acidity. Remember that a particular degree of level of acidity is needed for the correct activity of the enzymes and, therefore, for a great result of the final item.

- Presence of sugars. The sugars, which luckily are naturally in all flours, are fundamental in that they constitute the nutrition for the yeast. That's why often a percentage of malt, sugar or honey is contributed to the preliminary dough: it makes the activation of the yeast faster.

Tips and techniques for a best leavening

- Use a flour appropriate to the kind of dough and the leavening (the longer the leavening, the more powerful the chosen flour should be).
- Hold a temperature between 22-25°C and 28-30°C.

- Avoid sudden modifications in temperature level and drafts (better cover the bowl with a tidy tea towel and let it grow in a protected location).
- Calculate the leavening times as best you can to avoid that the dough growing too much.

RECIPES

Master Bread Recipe

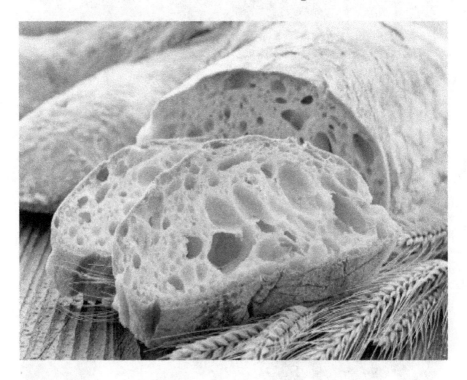

Traditionally, bread has actually been an essential food with almost ubiquitous consumption worldwide; it constitutes an essential source of energy and offers most nutrients and important micronutrients.

With the standard bread dough, in truth, you can make a lot of preparations, including pies, cakes and pizzas as well as lots of varieties of breads, buns and loaves with the addition of seeds or different flavorings.

There really is absolutely nothing quite like a warm slice of fresh bread served with butter on top. Mmmmm! This recipe is ideal. It's simple to follow, takes about a few hours to make and yields 2 loaves of wonderful bread. When it's out of the oven and partly cooled, everybody will thank you.

Ingredients

400 Calories Per Serving

- Manitoba flour 150 g.
- 00 Flour 350 g.
- Room temperature water 350 ml.
- Fresh brewer's yeast 7 g.
- Salt 8 g.
- Malt (or sugar or honey in the same doses) 1 tbsp.

Preparation

- The first thing to do when preparing the bread dough, start by liquifying the fresh brewer's yeast in the water at room temperature level.
- Mix together the flour into a big bowl and add 1 teaspoon of malt.
- Start mixing with one hand and with the other hand, pour the water little by little (add about half of it) then finally add the salt.
- Keep kneading and be pouring the water bit by bit, as you continue to knead. When you have actually also added the last part of water, continue to knead inside the bowl for about 10 minutes, until the dough is tightly strung.
- Starting from a moderate speed and increasing it somewhat to the end, you can make use of these steps using a mixer geared up with a hook. At this point, let the dough rest for about 10 minutes, it is not important to cover it.
- When the dough is well relaxed, move it to a lightly floured surface.
- Use your hands to spread the dough, then fold 2 of the 4 outer flaps towards the center.
- Fold the other two strips of dough towards the center and turn the bread upside down. Then shape the dough to offer it a round shape.
- Then transfer it to a gently floured bowl, cover with cling wrap and let rise for about 2 hours or at least till it is doubled. If the temperature level is rather high, simply leave it in the kitchen, away from drafts; in winter season, on the other hand, it is suggested to let the dough increase in the oven that is shut off only with the light on.
- At this moment, move the dough to a gently floured surface and duplicate the very same operations as previously.
- Fold it, then turn it upside down.

- As quickly as you have acquired a round shape, move it to a previously floured oven tray, cover with a moist cloth and let it rise for another hour.
- When it has increased well, preheat the oven to 250°C and utilizing a knife make decorative incisions. At this point, reduce the temperature level of the oven to 230°C and place a bowl filled with water on the bottom, it will assist to promote the ideal humidity.
- Bake the bread in the central shelf and cook for 20 minutes, then lower the temperature level to 180°C, remove the bowl of water and continue cooking for another 35 minutes.
- Once baked, let it cool prior to slicing!

Storage

Bread can be kept for 2-3 days in a paper bag. You can freeze it for about 1 month.

Baguette

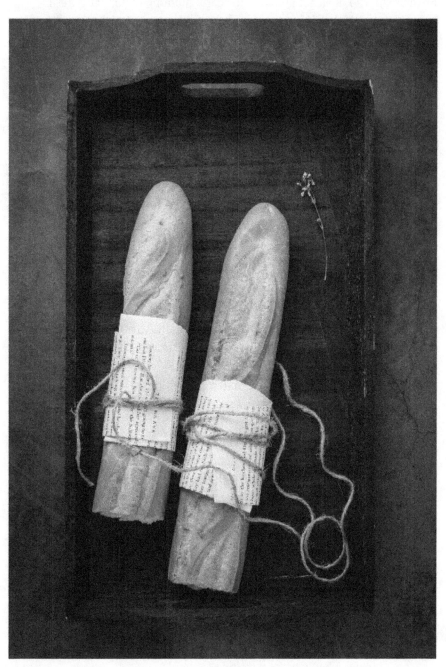

The baguette is a French bread famous all over the world. There is no Frenchman who does not go out in the early morning to purchase fresh baguette from the baker in his area. These baguettes taste rich, elegant, fragile, and yet, they have an exposed rough side. Crunchy on the outside, chewy on the inside.

Ingredients

Serving For 4 Baguettes:

- 00 Flour 500 g.
- Water 300 ml.
- Fresh brewer's yeast 10 g.
- Salt 15g.

Preparation

- Start by liquifying the fresh brewer's yeast in the water at room temperature level.
- Mix the flour into a big bowl and add the salt. After that add the yeast
- Knead well and cover the dough with a tea towel and let it increase for about one hour.
- After this time, move the dough to a gently floured surface, work it for a few minutes, and fold it several times on itself.
- Let rise for about 30 minutes.
- At this moment, split the dough into 4 pieces. The classic baguette should be about 70 cm long, about 5 wide and more or less 4 cm high). Place the baguettes on a floured sheet, well-spaced from each other by the folds of the cloth and let increase for another half an hour.
- In the meanwhile, preheat the oven at 230°C.
- Before baking, make cuts along the area of the baguettes with a blade and spray water on them.
- Lower the oven to 210°C and bake the baguettes at this temperature level for 30 minutes. When the baguette begins to brown, open the oven door a couple of times, so the steam clears and the surface of the bread dries to produce the crust. Switch off the oven and leave the baguettes for another 10 minutes; then take them out of the oven and let them cool on a rack: the baguettes are waiting for you!

Tips

You can coat the baguettes with poppy seeds or sesame seeds, brushing the surface area with oil prior to baking them.

Ciabatta

Authentic ciabatta has a rustic appearance; however, it is surprisingly soft and chewy. The high hydration in this bread results in a wonderfully chewy center and lots of irregular holes. The dough is characterized by a high percentage of water on the amount of the flour, long leavening times and by the presence of a pre-dough, the poolish, which rests and ferments for a couple of hours and then is kneaded again by adding additional water, salt, yeast and malt until a soft but well-cohesive dough is obtained.

Before you make this ciabatta recipe, understand that the dough can be challenging to manage properly. It's wet. Don't include extra flour or you'll get frustrating outcomes. Simply rest guaranteed that, as you make the dough again and again, you'll end up being practiced in how to manage it.

Ingredients

200 Calories Per Serving, Dosages For 10 Ciabatta

For the poolish:

- Manitoba flour 200 g.
- 00 flour 100 g.
- Water 300 ml.
- Dry brewer's yeast 2 g.

For the dough:

- Manitoba flour 400 g.
- 00 flour 200 g.
- Water 350 ml.
- Dry brewer's yeast 3 g.
- Malt 10 g.
- Salt 20 g.

Poolish Preparation:

- To prepare the ciabatta, start kneading the poolish, a very hydrated yeast: liquify the dry brewer's yeast in the water (you can even use 6 g

of fresh brewer's yeast); in a bowl blend the two sieved flours, the 00 flour and the manitoba, then add everything by pouring the liquid on the flours.
- Mix well with a wooden spoon until a homogeneous, really soft and smooth dough is obtained. Cover the dough with cling wrap and let it increase for about 3 hours at room temperature.

Second dough preparation:

- You can now proceed with the 2nd dough: dissolve the dry brewer's yeast (alternatively, you can utilize 9 g of fresh brewer's yeast) and the malt (or sugar) in the water, mix together the sorted flours and pour the poolish into the bowl of an electric mixer, equipped with a flat beater. If you do not have it, you can knead it in a bowl aided by a spoon initially, and after that, once all the components have actually been gathered, continue with your hands.
- While the mixer is running at medium speed, include alternating, both the liquid and the powders, until ended up. When all the ingredients are gathered around the flat beater, tidy it, and change it with the hook. Continue to knead like this for 5 minutes, add salt and continue for another 8 minutes, till the dough has twisted around the hook.
- At that point, detach it and move it to a bowl (or leave it directly in the used cup), cover it with cling wrap and let it rest for 1 hour at room temperature level, preferably between 24 and 25 degrees.
- After this time, turn the dough upside down on a floured work surface and continue to practise the folds that will then be utilized for the leavening: bring the dough forward, then fold the lower part on the upper part and after that fold laterally on one side and on the other.
- Somewhat flatten the dough and divide it into 10 pieces, which will each weigh about 150-160 g.
- Let the dough rise on a well-floured surface area. Cover with cling wrap, to avoid the surface area dough from drying out and leave them for at least 1 hour in a warm environment. After this time, the loaves will double in volume.
- Now take one loaf at a time, turn it upside down and move it instantly onto a baking tray currently heated up in the oven. Stretch the dough, pulling it gently, so as not to let the leavening gases getaway and bake

them. Preheat the oven at 240-250°C.
- Cooking is the trickiest stage: for the first 10 minutes, the ciabatta needs to bake at 240-250°C. After the first 10 minutes, lower the temperature level to 200°C and cook for another 10 minutes. Continue cooking for the last 3-4 minutes, keeping the oven ajar with a wooden spoon embedded in the opening, to create an air vent and to release excess steam, so as to favour cooking and get a crunchy texture. Then cool your ciabatta in a rack and enjoy it.

Bagel

Bagels are sandwiches with a classic donut shape, covered with poppy or sesame seeds and stuffed in a classic way with salmon and cream cheese or according to taste. The bagels are also exceptionally light because they are not fried, but first boiled and then baked in the oven. Ideal for lunch in the office or for a dinner with friends, the bagels are also perfect for Sunday brunch or for a picnic on beautiful spring days. They are suitable for any occasion.

Ingredients

Dosage for 6 Bagels

- 00 flour 350 g.
- Water 200 ml.
- Dry brewer's yeast 4 g.
- Salt 6 g.
- Malt 10 g.
- Sesame or Poppy seeds.

Preparation

- To prepare the bagels, mix the flour in a bowl, then add the dry beer yeast and the malt.
- Add the water and knead with your hands; once a homogeneous mixture is obtained, you can add the salt and continue working until it is completely absorbed.
- At this point, transfer the mixture onto a pastry board and knead it for about 5-6 minutes until you obtain a smooth and homogeneous mixture; then place it in a large bowl, cover with cling film for food and leave to rise for about 4 hours and a temperature of 28-30°C.
- Once the dough has tripled in volume, transfer it back to the pastry board and with your hands, make a strand.
- From this, obtain 6 pieces of 90 g each. Using the palm of your hand, transform each piece into a ball, applying light pressure against the pastry board and twirling. Repeat described to form all 6 balls, then cover with a kitchen towel and let stand for ten minutes.
- At this point, placing your fingers in the center of each sphere and spreading them outwards you can obtain your donuts, with a diameter of

about 10 cm. Manually place the bagels on a tray, then let it rise for another 40-50 minutes always and a temperature of 28-30°C or in the oven turned off only with the light on, until it is doubled in volume. Meanwhile, place a pan with water on the heat and bring to the boil.
- Cook the bagels in the boiling water for about 20 seconds per side, then drain them and place them on a baking sheet
- Cover the surface with sesame seeds and bake in a preheated oven at 220°C for 30 minutes. Once cooked and golden brown, take them out of the oven and let them cool before serving.

Bretzel

Bretzel is a particular type of bread with a knotted shape and a golden and shiny crust covered with grains of salt. It is widespread in countries such as Germany and Austria. They can be found in a large, small, simple version, flavored with spices! Slightly crunchy on the outside, soft on the inside and with an unmistakable flavor, they go very well with beer.

Ingredients

300 Calories Per Serving, Dosage for 8 Bretzel

For the pre-fermented yeast:

- Water 55 ml
- 00 flour 100 g.
- Sugar 12 g.
- Dry brewer's yeast 4 g.

For the bretzel:

- 00 flour 400 g.
- Water 215 ml.
- Butter 50 g.
- Salt 12 g.
- Baking soda 30 g.
- Salt flakes to season.

Pre-Fermented Yeast Preparation:

- To prepare the bretzels, start by preparing the yeast: take a bowl and liquify the yeast in warm water, add the sugar, mix and then add it to the flour.
- Place the dough in a bowl, cover with cling wrap and let it increase in the oven shut off with the light on for at least 1 hour until the dough has actually doubled its volume.

Bretzel Preparation:

- Liquify the salt in the water, put the flour in a bowl, including the water in which you have liquified the salt, the yeast, the softened butter into small pieces and knead vigorously with your hands till a smooth and homogeneous mixture is acquired.
- Place the dough in a bowl, cover and let it increase in the oven with the light on for several hours. When the dough has actually risen, knead the mix once again on a gently floured surface area.

- At this point, divides the dough into eight equivalent parts and provide it with the shape of cables about 50 cm long, leaving completions narrower than the center, fold the two ends down.
- Then provide the cord with the typical "slow knot" shape by crossing the two ends and folding them on edge.
- Once you have formed your bretzels, put them on a floured cloth and let rise for 30 minutes. Then put them in the refrigerator to rest for an hour. Meanwhile, boil 4 liters of water, and when it has boiled, add three tablespoons of baking soda.
- Helping yourself with a slotted spoon, lay the bretzel, no greater than two at a time, in water until they are glossy (30 -40 seconds). Drain them and place on fabric to dry the excess water.
- Place the bretzels on a baking tray, then sprinkle them with coarse salt (or flakes) over the entire surface.
- Bake the bretzels for 20 minutes in the oven preheated to 220°C and then took them out of the oven when they become brown.
- Let the bretzels cool down and then enjoy them.

Advice

You can customize your bretzels by garnishing them with poppy or sesame seeds rather of salt.

Entire Grain Bread

Wholemeal Sandwiches

When you prepare your bread, you get this alluring scent that emanates when freshly baked is truly delicious and spreads gradually throughout our home! In this recipe, we provide the wholemeal sandwiches, small tasty and light sandwiches prepared with wholemeal flour. This bread is best to accompany your meal and suitable to serve with various kinds of fillings.

Ingredients

150 Calories Per Serving, Doses for 20 pieces.

- Manitoba flour 500 g.
- Wholemeal flour 300 g.
- Lukewarm water 640 ml.
- Salt 20 g.
- Dry brewer's yeast 8 g.
- Flax seeds 30 g.
- Extra virgin olive oil.

Preparation

- To prepare the wholemeal bread rolls, sift the manitoba flour in a bowl, pour the entire wheat flour, the dry brewer's yeast and stir with a spoon.
- In a container, liquify the salt in warm water, then put the saltwater into the powders and mix with your hands.
- Knead again extremely quickly: the dough should be sticky and very soft. Work it until you acquire a homogeneous consistency, then form a ball, place it in the bowl and cover with cling wrap. Leave it to rise for at least 1 hour. After the required time has elapsed, the dough will have swelled and doubled in volume. At this moment, make some folds to give the ideal increase to the leavening, keep kneading and then turn it and form a ball.
- Cover once again with cling film, letting it rest for another hour in the oven, turned off with the light on. After that time, take the dough (which meanwhile will have risen) and make some folds again to make it more flexible, working it on an oiled work surface area.
- Split the dough into 20 portions weighing 70 g each. With your hands formed balls.
- Let it rise again for 1 hour.
- Bake in the oven at 190°C for 30 minutes, finally you can get and serve your wholemeal sandwiches.

Whole Grain Loaf

Whole wheat bread, prepared with bran-rich flour, is an excellent substitute for white bread as it is rich in fiber, vitamins and minerals. This bread is totally made with wholemeal flour, which, compared to the normal one, contains some difficulties of preparation, especially in the leavening phase, less than the ordinary one. The result, however, will be that of excellent bread, soft and with numerous properties given by the use of wholemeal flour.

Ingredients

290 calories per serving

- Wholemeal flour 500 g.
- Water 350 ml.
- Fresh brewer's yeast 12 g.
- Salt 10 g.
- Extra Virgin Olive Oil 3 tbsp.
- Malt 1 tbsp.

Preparation

- To make wholemeal bread, first in a small bowl, blend to liquefy the brewer's yeast with warm water (taking it from what you have available as per the recipe). Add the malt (or sugar) and dissolve everything. In the remaining water, dissolve the salt and add the oil. Pour the wholemeal flour into a bowl, then add the yeast mixture and also add the water with the dissolved salt and oil.
- Knead well for at least 8-10 minutes until a homogeneous mixture is obtained. Brush a bowl with oil and place the obtained dough inside.
- Cover with cling wrap and leave to rise for at least 1 hour and a half or two. The dough will have to double its volume.
- After that time, take the dough and knead it until you get a loaf. Place the wholemeal bread on a baking sheet lined with baking paper and cover it with a glass bowl or cling wrap and let it rise again until doubled in volume.
- When the bread is ready, make transversal cuts with the knife on the surface and bake it in a preheated oven at 180°C for about 45-50 minutes. Remove the whole wheat bread from the oven when it is slightly golden on the surface!

Advice

The wholemeal bread can be kept for about 2 days covered with cling wrap.

Multi Cereal Bread

Cereal bread is delicious and rich in fiber. It is a good alternative to whole wheat bread and is easily digestible. It is excellent as breakfast, with jam or butter on top, or with any meal of the day.

In this recipe, I will explain step by step how to make this delicious bread with your own hands.

Ingredients

200 CALORIES PER SERVING

- Manitoba flour 150 g.
- Whole wheat flour 75 g.
- Whole spelled flour 75 g.
- Water 205 ml.
- Dry brewer's yeast 1,5 g.

- Honey 5 g.
- Salt 8 g.
- Mixed seeds 60 g.

Preparation

- To prepare the cereal bread, start to mixing the manitoba flour, the entire wheat flour and also the spelled flour together in a bowl.
- Include the yeast and honey. Mix and add water at room temperature. Mix well for at least 10 minutes.
- When you have gotten a uniform mixture to add the seeds, knead for about 2 minutes to mix them with the dough.
- Lastly, put the salt and continue to knead for another 5 minutes.
- Gather the dough gotten, giving it the shape of a ball and place it in a big bowl. Let increase for about 1 hour and a half.
- As soon as the leavening time has expired, the dough should have doubled in volume. Transfer it to a lightly floured pastry board and spread it slightly with your hands.
- Let it increase for at least 1 hour. At this moment, the bread will be doubled in volume.
- After that time, spray the surface area with 10 g of mixed seeds. Preheat the oven at 180°C and bake the cereal bread. After 45 minutes, it will be ready, take it out of the oven, slice it and bring to the table still steaming!

Special Bread

Olive Bread

Olive bread is a tasty alternative to classic white bread. It is a soft bread enriched with green olives, cut into small pieces, which make it delicious even alone.

Ingredients

Pre-fermented yeast:

- Manitoba flour 100 g.
- Water 75 ml.
- Fresh brewer's yeast 2,5 g.

For the dough:

- Manitoba Flour 500 g.
- Water 300 ml.
- Fresh brewer's yeast 15 g.
- Malt 10 g.
- Salt 10 g.
- Olives 200 g.

Pre-Fermented Yeast Preparation:

- Preparing the olive bread begins by preparing the pre-fermented yeast. Liquify in a small bowl the fresh brewer's yeast with warm water and then add flour and the salt. Knead for a few seconds and then cover the bowl with cling wrap and let it rise for about 1 hour and a half at room temperature. In that time, the pre-fermented yeast must double its volume.

Dough Preparation:

- In a small bowl, liquify the brewer's yeast and dissolve it with warm water (taken from the dose of the recipe) together with the malt (or honey).
- Place the flour in a bowl, add the yeast mixture, the remaining water and knead for about 10 minutes. After that time, add the pre-fermented yeast

to the dough and keep kneading for another 10 minutes until the mixture is homogeneous. When it is ready, add the chopped olives and mix for a few seconds.
- Shape the dough and let it rise until doubled in volume.
- Preheat the oven at 180°C and bake the olive bread for at least 40 minutes. When the surface is golden brown, it can be removed from the oven and left to cool on a rack.

Advice

You can try this recipe adding to the dough with dried tomatoes and capers.

Walnuts Bread

Getting your hands in the dough is a real natural anti-stress activity that will permit you to get fresh bread to bring to the table every day, with the awareness of the ingredients used. Making bread in your home is constantly enchanting, the flour that flutters all over and the scent that spreads out quickly throughout makes this minute truly magical. So what are you waiting for? Fasten your aprons and prepare the walnut bread. There is absolutely nothing better than a slice of a still steaming loaf!

Ingredients

395 calories per serving

- 00 flour 300 g.
- Wholemeal flour 200 g.
- Water 350 ml.
- Dry brewer's yeast 3 g.
- Salt 10 g.

- Walnut kernels 100 g.

Preparation

- To prepare the walnut bread, start with chopping the walnuts and keep them aside. Now take care of making the dough: include the flours inside a bowl, mix and add the dry brewer's yeast and the water.
- Knead for 8-10 minutes. Only at this moment, you can include salt and walnuts.
- Once the nuts and salt are well incorporated, transfer the dough onto a lightly floured pastry board.
- Helped by your hands, give the dough a round shape and put it inside a bowl.
- Cover with cling wrap and let it rise for 3,5 hours. Once it has doubled its volume, transfer the dough onto a lightly floured pastry board.
- Fold the dough once again and give the bread the shape of a loaf, then move it to a baking sheet and let it rise for another hour.
- Create the traditional cuts on the surface area of the bread with a knife.
- Bake the walnut bread for 40 minutes at 220°C. As soon as baked, let your walnut bread cool before slicing and serve

Pumpkin Bread

All seasons have their representative ingredients. When we refer to fall and winter, one of the main ingredients is pumpkin. With a delicate and neutral flavor, this bread is perfect for any meal of the day. Once you try it, you can't do without it.

Ingredients

350 calories per serving

- 00 flour 500 g.
- Dry brewer's yeast 4 g.
- Water 100 ml.
- Salt 10 g.
- Pumpkin 400 g.
- Extra virgin olive oil 20 ml.

- Pumpkin seeds 15 g.

Preparation

- To prepare this bread, start by cleaning the pumpkin: eliminate the seeds and internal filaments and cut into little pieces, and likewise eliminate the peel.
- Place a pan with water on the stove and cook the pumpkin wedges for about 30 minutes, it must be soft. You can inspect its consistency with a fork.
- Pass the prepared pulp with a stick mixer to obtain a puree.
- In a large bowl place, the flour then add the pumpkin puree and the yeast.
- Mix for at least 10 minutes. When the dough is nearly ready, you can include salt: do not add it before because if inserted too early, it would prevent the dough from increasing. Keep kneading for 2-3 minutes more, then add the oil.
- Transfer the dough to the work surface area and fold it. Shape the dough and form a ball. Cover with cling film and let the dough rise for at least 3 hours.
- After that time, gently flour the work surface and put the leavened dough into it and do the same: form a well-sealed ball as previously and position it on the baking tray covered with a kitchen towel.
- Let rise for another 1 hour then, with a knife make eight cuts on the surface area of the dough, to make it comparable to a real pumpkin.
- At this moment, disperse the pumpkin seeds inside the grooves you have sculpted.
- Bake the bread at 200°C for 55 minutes
- Let your pumpkin bread cool off before enjoying it!

Storage

As you know, the bread is good fresh: if possible, consume it throughout the day. You can keep it in a paper bag for about 3 days. You can also freeze pumpkin bread.

Tricolor Bread

This simple recipe of homemade tricolor bread will allow, even the less experienced, to amaze their guests with a chromatic and fragrant loaf. It is an alternative concept to enrich the breadbasket, to taste it alone or as a base for tasty sandwiches!

Ingredients

- Manitoba flour 175 g.
- 00 flour 150 g.
- Eggs 1.
- Dry brewer's yeast 2 g.
- Tomato paste 15 g.

- Spinach 70 g.
- Softened butter 75 g.
- Water 250 ml
- Salt 5 g.

Preparation

- To prepare the tricolor bread, liquify the dry brewer's yeast in a little warm water (taken from the 250 ml required for the dough).
- Stir with a teaspoon and include the mixture to the sifted flour and pour into the bowl. Mix the components, then include the egg and the dosage of warm water showed for the mix.
- Continue to knead and when the mix is uniform, put the salt. Work the dough and add the softened butter into little pieces.
- Knead the dough for at least 10 minutes until it is homogeneous and smooth.
- Transfer it into a bowl, cover with cling film and let increase for at least 2 hours (it will need to double its volume).
- Meanwhile, clean the spinach and stew it in a pan with a drizzle of oil covered with a lid. Once cooked, let cool and after that pour into mixer, include 20 ml of water and whisk until a velvety mixture is obtained.
- Then take back the dough that will have doubled its volume transfer it to a gently oiled work surface and divide it into 3 parts (you can wrap the ones you are not utilizing at the moment) and season one with the spinach, kneading to blend them homogeneously.
- Then season the last part of the dough with tomato paste.
- Proceed in the very same method and form with the 3 parts a braid. Cover with cling film and leave to rise for at least 30 minutes. After the needed time, bake the tricolor bread in a preheated oven at 200°C for about 60 minutes.
- Examine the cooking with a toothpick before finishing cooking; when the tricolor bread is cooked, take it out of the oven and let it cool.

Storage

You can keep the tricolor bread in a frost bag for food for 1-2 days. You can freeze the dough after the very first leavening and, if needed, defrost it in the refrigerator and bring it to room temperature level.

Classic Bread

Grissini

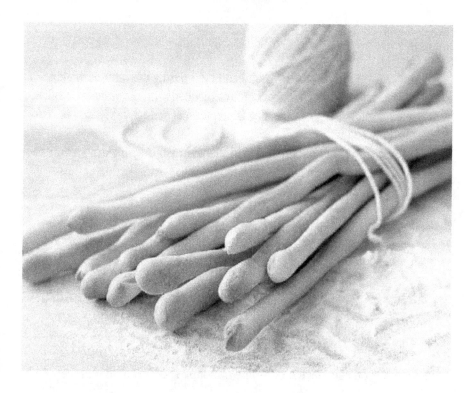

The breadsticks are the popular crispy and lengthened loaves of bread from Italy. Known and munched all over the world, they are among the finest understood Italian gastronomic products abroad. The consumption of these tasty elongated loaves, initially a benefit of the nobles, soon infected the entire population!

Ingredients

Dosage for 40 Grissini

- 00 Flour 500 g.
- Fresh brewer's yeast 15 g.
- Water 280 ml.
- Salt 8 g.

- Extra virgin olive oil 50 ml.

Preparation

- To prepare the breadsticks, start by liquifying the brewer's yeast in the water.
- Put the sorted flour in a bowl and add the mixture of water with yeast. Mix and also include the oil you have blended with the water and salt.
- Knead until an elastic substance is acquired. Then move the dough onto a pastry board.
- Forming the dough into a rectangle shape, brush it with extra virgin olive oil. Then let the dough increase till it has actually doubled its initial volume.
- After the time needed for the leavening (about 1 hour), with a long knife cut the dough for the brief side into strips of about 1 cm each.
- Grab each strip of dough with both hands and pull it up until it reaches the length of the tray you will use to bake them.
- Arrange the breadsticks well apart from each other on a baking tray lined with baking paper and cook them at 200°C for about 20 minutes.

Advice

If you desire, you can place the sesame or poppy seeds straight into the dough.

Piadina

Piadina, also known as flatbread, is a typical product of Italian street food. Soft, thin and very easy to prepare... Excellent for a snack or any meal of the day. You can fill it with whatever you like: ham, fresh mozzarella and salad. Be creative!

Ingredients

- Dosage for 6 Piadina
- 00 flour 500 g.
- Water 170 ml.
- Baking soda 1,5 tbsp.
- Lard 125 g.
- Salt 15 g.

Preparation

- To make the piadina, prepare the dough by mixing the flour, salt, lard and baking soda in a bowl.
- Knead and add the water 3 times, then transfer the dough to the work surface and continue working until you obtain a homogeneous mixture. Form a ball, wrap it in a food bag and let it rise for 30 minutes.
- After the rest time, remove the dough from the bag and form a sausage, then divide it into 6 equal portions. Give each portion of the dough the shape of a ball by working it for about 30 seconds so it becomes smooth and uniform, then wrap it again with a food bag and let it rest for another 30 minutes.
- After the rest time, lightly flour the work surface and roll the balls with a rolling pin up to a thickness of 2-3 mm. Heat a pan well and meanwhile cut the piadinas in a round shape.
- Now cook the piadinas on one side for 2 minutes, rotating them continuously with one hand to ensure uniform cooking, then turn them and cook for 2 minutes on the other side as well, until they are lightly browned.
- Once cooked, stack your piadinas one on top of the other and fill them still hot!

Original Focaccia

Tall and soft, with olives or tomatoes, there are many different types of focaccia in Italian cuisine. The original focaccia recipe involves the use of flour, yeast, water, oil and salt. Still, you can add various ingredients to the dough to make it even richer and more aromatic. For starters, we'll show you a recipe for Genovese focaccia.

Ingredients

- Manitoba Flour 330 g.
- Fresh brewer's yeast 13 g.
- Water 225 ml.
- Extra virgin olive oil 25 ml.
- Salt 5 g.

Preparation

- To prepare the focaccia, start by crumbling the fresh yeast with the flour in a little bowl, add half of the water and mix.
- Mix for about 5 minutes and gradually add the rest of the water. When it is completely absorbed, add the salt.
- Then include the oil and continue to knead until you see that the dough has taken a consistency and is homogeneous.
- Transfer the dough into a bowl and cover with cling film. Let it increase for 3 hours.
- After that time, take a tray (I used a rectangle-shaped tray 35x28) lined with baking paper and carefully brushing the entire surface with oil, put the mix inside and grease your hands so as not to stick the dough.
- Spread it with your fingertips till it covers the surface area and sides.
- Being a hydrated dough, if you cannot fill the whole mold instantly, let it rest for a couple of minutes before continuing to spread out the dough.
- Sprinkle with the oil, a few leaves of rosemary and salt flakes. Your focaccia is ready to be cooked in the oven at 210°C for about 20 minutes.

Storage

To ensure you taste the focaccia much better, I suggest consuming it at the minute. But it can be kept for as much as 2 days by keeping it closed in a bag;

in this case it is advised to heat the focaccia in the oven for a few minutes.

Sweetened Bread

Brioches Bread

Brioche is a bread of French origin light and puffy, ideal for breakfast. You can fill with jam, custard or spread hazelnut. Try Brioche bread in the morning with coffee. It's perfect for starting your day in the best way.

Ingredients (for a 26X11 cm mold)

- 00 flour 260 g.
- Fresh brewer's yeast 8 g.
- Milk 20 ml.
- Eggs 2.
- Sugar 25 g.
- Butter 135 g.

- Salt 5 g.

To brush

- Yolk 1.

Preparation

- To prepare the brioche, start by weighing all the active ingredients, remembering that they need to all be at room temperature to guarantee the best results. In a bowl place the flour, add the crumbled brewer's yeast and the sugar.
- Mix and then add the slightly beaten eggs, putting them gradually, this permitting the dough to absorb them slowly. Do the same with the milk. Keep working until a compact dough is formed.
- After that time, put the softened butter, this too, bit by bit, waiting on a piece to be absorbed before adding the next. Just at the end, include salt.
- At this point, you will need to continue working the dough for about 20 minutes.
- Transfer the dough to a newly floured work surface area and knead it for 1-2 minutes and after that put into a container and cover with cling wrap.
- At this point, the dough will need to rise for about 2 hours.
- After the time, transfer the dough onto a gently floured pastry board and form a loaf, simply by gently pulling the dough with your hands. From this, you get 8 pieces of about 70 grams each, cutting them with a knife.
- Place the balls in a buttered plumcake mold of 26x11 cm, organizing them in 2 rows.
- Let rise it for about 2 and a half hours till they have actually reached half of the mold.
- Brush with a beaten egg yolk and bake, in a preheated oven, at 170°C for about 35 minutes.
- You can serve it in slices to spread out jams or hazelnut cream or whatever you like!

Storage

The brioche bread dries very quickly, so keep it constantly in a food bag, and consume it in 1-2 days. You can prepare the dough the night before: when you come to the first leavening, let it rise for an hour and after that put it in the fridge overnight. The next day, enable to acclimatize for a couple of hours and continue with the recipe. You can freeze the brioche once cooked and cooled completely, possibly sliced so regarding thaw as required.

Banana Bread

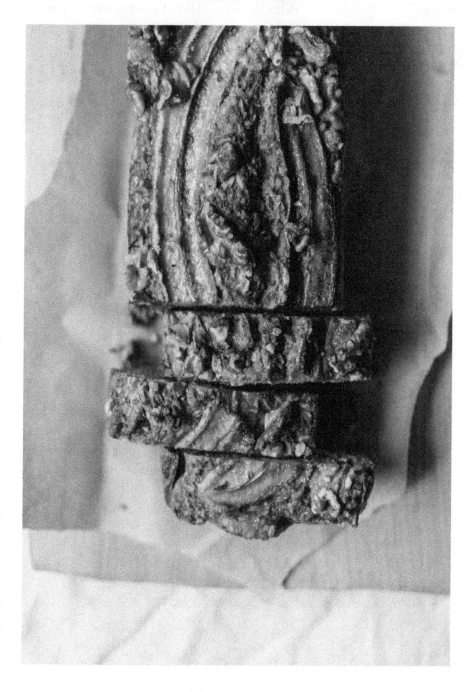

Banana bread is a typical breakfast for many of us. Quick and easy to prepare, it is likewise a way to use those bananas that are frequently forgotten in the fruit basket, too ripe to be enjoyed in purity. Try this version of banana bread and enrich it to taste with coarsely sliced chocolate walnuts or hazelnuts. It will be even much better!

Ingredients (for a 22.5 x 8.5 cm mold)

- Bananas (the pulp of about 4 bananas) 450 g.
- 00 flour 200 g.
- Butter 120 g.
- Sugar 120 g.
- Eggs 2.
- Cinnamon powder 1/2 tbsp.
- Baking powder for cakes 6 g.
- Baking Soda 3 g.
- Lemon juice
- Salt

Preparation

- To prepare the banana bread, start by peeling the bananas and cutting them into slices.
- Put them into a bowl and drizzle with lemon juice to prevent blackening.
- Mash them with a fork to minimize them to puree and set aside.
- In another bowl, put the butter into little pieces and sugar. Work with an electrical whisk and when you have acquired a homogeneous mixture, add the eggs, one at a time to incorporate them better.
- Include a pinch of salt, then pour the banana puree.
- Mix with a spoon and continue combining the flour with baking soda and baking powder. Season with cinnamon and mix once again.
- Put the dough into the 22.5 x8.5 cm mold and level it. Bake in a preheated oven at 180°C for about 1 hour.
- Enjoy the banana bread alone or accompanied by butter, peanut butter or jams.

Advice

You can flavor banana bread with vanilla instead of cinnamon, include chocolate chips or coarsely sliced walnuts or almonds!

Raisin Bread

Raisin bread is ideal for improving the rich Christmas menu. The unique flavour, slightly sweet, it is exceptional when accompanied by cheeses and honey. With this simple recipe, you will amaze your guests.

Ingredients

- Manitoba flour 300 g.
- 00 Flour 200 g.
- Fresh brewer's yeast 25 g.
- Milk 300 ml.
- Sugar 2 tbsp.
- Raisins 350 g.

Preparation

- In a large bowl, soak the raisins for thirty minutes.
- At the end of this time, into a big bowl, put in the milk, the brewer yeast and then add the flours and knead for at least 10 minutes. When the dough forms include the sugar and work until the dough is smooth and homogeneous, at this moment add the well-squeezed raisins, let it blend well and end up the dough.
- Place the dough in a container, cover it with a kitchen towel, and let increase for about 1 hour or at least till doubled.
- After that time, transfer the dough to a work surface and lightly wet the bread surface with milk and sprinkle abundantly with sugar.
- Preheat the oven to 180°C and bake the bread for 40 minutes.

PIZZA RECIPES

Pizza Dough

Nowadays, Italian pizza is known all over the world. Thanks to its simplicity and the few necessary ingredients, it is very quick to make and is a delicious meal that everyone likes. There are many different methods, ingredients and toppings, but the basic recipe consists of a few genuine ingredients: flour, yeast, salt and water. In this recipe, I will teach you how to make pizza dough in your home. Let's start!

Ingredients

- Manitoba flour 100 g.
- 00 flour 150 g.
- Water 150 ml.
- Fresh brewer's yeast 5 g.
- Extra virgin olive oil 20 ml.
- Salt 5 g.

Preparation

- Start by putting the yeast into the water and dissolve it well.
- Continue by pouring the Manitoba and 00 flour into a container.
- Pour the water gradually while kneading with your hands: the perfect water temperature is 25°C. You can also add salt when you have poured half the liquid and continue to blend, putting the water a little at a time until a uniform mixture is acquired.
- At this point, you can include the oil, this too, poured gradually while continuing to knead.
- Move the dough to the work surface area and work it with your hands till it is smooth and homogeneous.
- As soon as you have a nice smooth dough, let it rest for about 10 minutes. As soon as it rests, give it a small cut. Imagine the sphere is divided into 4 parts, take the end of each one, gently pull it out and fold it towards the center, then give it a ball shape.
- Transfer the dough formed into a bowl, cover with a cloth and allow to rise for about 2 hours.
- After that time, place the dough in a tray and spread it with your fingertips till it covers the surface area and sides.

- Season the pizza as you want!

Storage

When leavened, pizza dough can also be frozen, ideally divided into portions, and stored in a frost bag.

If you choose, you can also freeze the semi-cooked pizza: simply prepare it midway, let it cool and finally freeze it covered with aluminum; then just cook it, still frozen, at a slightly lower temperature level.

Ideas for replacing flours

All flours absorb in different ways, therefore altering the proposed mix or using various flours implies needing to change in a different way with the liquids. Additionally, the outcome will always differ. So if you want to change the recipe, the only option is: try it to find the winning mix!

This little paragraph allows you to make a healthy and soft pizza dough by using other types of flours: Whole Wheat and Gluten-Free.

Table 1: The recipes are for a single (1) portion.

WHOLE WHEAT	GLUTEN FREE
- Whole Wheat flour: 125 g - Flour "0": 125 g	- Rice flour: 175 g - Corn starch: 125 g
- Dry brewer's yeast: 2 g	- Fresh brewer's yeast: 12 g
- Water: 150 ml	- Water: 175 ml
- EVO: 20 ml	- EVO: 20 ml
- Salt: 5 g	- Salt: 5 g

N.B.: make sure you knead the dough for at least 5 minutes.

In this way, you let the right amount of air to be incorporated into your dough. That's a guarantee of great results.

Tips

For cooking pizza dough, remember there is no fixed rule. In general, it is advisable to understand that the oven needs to be extremely hot before baking the pizza. The perfect temperature is between 200°C and 250°C, times vary according to the temperature.

PIZZA TOPPING

Marinara

The original Marinara is an explosion of simplicity and flavors.

→ Marinara Sauce (Tomato + Garlic)

→ Oregano

→ Fresh Basil

→ Extra Virgin Olive Oil (EVO)

Margherita

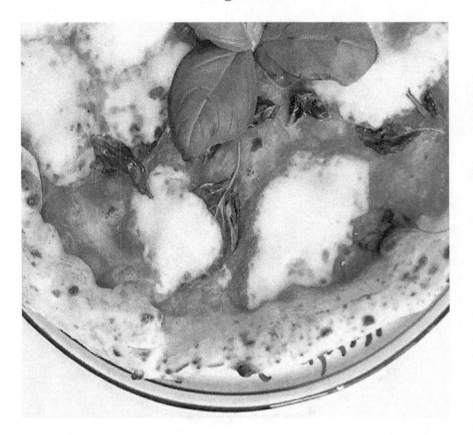

Dedicated to the Queen Margherita, this pizza represents the colors of the Italian flag, red (tomato), white (mozzarella) and green (basil).

→ Tomato Sauce

→ Fior di latte (Mozzarella)

→ Fresh Basil

→ Extra Virgin Olive Oil (EVO)

Bufala

If you want something special but simple, the Bufala Pizza is the right one for you. Margherita Base topped with Buffalo Mozzarella DOP.

→ Tomato Sauce

→ Buffalo Mozzarella DOP (Bufala)

→ Fresh Basil

→ Extra Virgin Olive Oil (EVO)

Emilia Romagna

The essential flavour of Emilia Romagna region. Mortadella and local pistachios, an extraordinary couple for the most refined palates.

→ Fior di latte (Mozzarella)

→ Mortadella

→ Roasted Pistachios Pieces

→ Extra Virgin Olive Oil (EVO)

Lombardia

The ancient Original Gorgonzola taste warms your heart in the cold winter days—a delicacy for all palates.

→ Fior di latte (Mozzarella)

→ Gorgonzola Cheese DOP

→ Spinach

→ Parmesan Cheese

→ Fresh Basil

Trentino

One of the Italian people's favourite pizza. Speck with tasty cheese.

→ Tomato Sauce

→ Fior di latte (Mozzarella)

→ Speck

→ Brie Cheese

→ Fresh Basil

Liguria

The essence of Liguria Region: Homemade Pesto! This pizza is even perfect for vegetarians.

→ Fior di latte (Mozzarella)

→ Fresh Cherry Tomatoes

→ Homemade Pesto Sauce

→ Fresh Basil

Roma

...Also known as Carbonara, this pizza is the perfect reproduction of all the flavors of the Italian Capital.

→ Fior di latte (Mozzarella)

→ Scrambled Eggs

→ Guanciale (Bacon Pieces)

→ Pecorino Romano Cheese

→ Black Pepper & Fresh Basil

Sicilia

The flavor of the sea is enclosed here.

→ Tomato Sauce

→ Fior di latte (Mozzarella)

→ Black Olives

→ Anchovies

→ Fresh Basil

Puglia

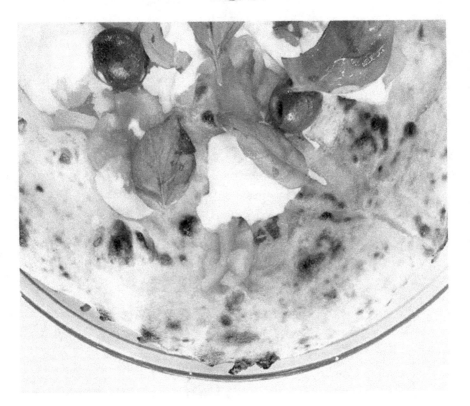

Fresh and Fragrant. It recalls the summer and all its memories.

→ Stracciatella Cheese

→ Yellow Cherry Tomatoes

→ Black Olives

→ Fresh Basil

→ Extra Virgin Olive Oil (EVO)

Abruzzo

The original flavour of the Abruzzo region. Those tasty ingredients make everyone happy.

→ Tomato Sauce

→ Fior di Latte (Mozzarella)

→ Guanciale (Bacon Pieces)

→ Pecorino Romano Cheese

→ Fresh Basil

→ Extra Virgin Olive Oil (EVO)

Piemonte

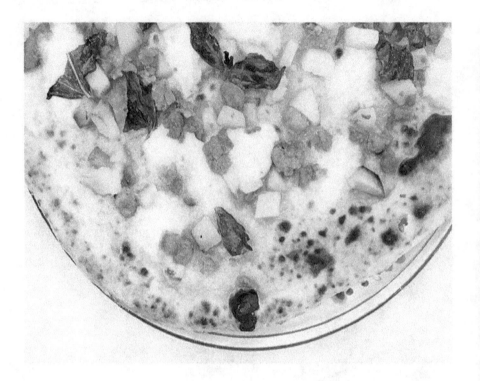

Directly from the Alps, this rustic pizza takes you into a new culinary experience.

- → Fior di Latte (Mozzarella)
- → Sausages Pieces
- → Baked Potatoes
- → Fresh Basil
- → Black Pepper (optional)

Toscana

Special pizza, typically for springtime, that will amaze your guests.

→ Fior di Latte (Mozzarella)

→ Crudo di Parma Ham

→ Fig Jam

→ Fresh Basil

MEASUREMENTS CONVERSION

OVEN TEMPERATURES	
CELSIUS (°C)	FAHRENHEIT(°F)
120	*250*
150	*300*
165	*325*
180	*350*
190	*375*
200	*400*
220	*425*
230	*450*

WEIGHT EQUIVALENTS		
METRIC	US STANDARD	US STANDARD
15 g	½ ounce	1 tbsp
30 g	1 ounce	2 tbsp
60 g	2 ounce	4 tbsp
115 g	4 ounce	8 tbsp
225 g	8 ounce	16 tbsp
340 g	12 ounce	24 tbsp
455 g	16 ounce = 1 pound	32 tbsp

www.ingramcontent.com/pod-product-compliance
Lightning Source LLC
LaVergne TN
LVHW091601230125
801996LV00011B/292